How to Negotiate Like a Pro

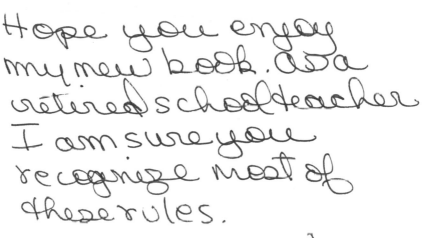

Mary

Hope you enjoy
my new book. As a
retired schoolteacher
I am sure you
recognize most of
these rules.

Happy negotiating

Love

Mary

How to Negotiate Like a Pro

✦

41 Rules for Resolving Disputes

Mary Greenwood, J.D., LL.M
Author of *Hiring, Supervising and
Firing Employees: An Employer's
Guide to Discrimination Laws*

iUniverse, Inc.
New York Lincoln Shanghai

How to Negotiate Like a Pro
41 Rules for Resolving Disputes

iUniverse books may be ordered through booksellers or by contacting:

iUniverse
2021 Pine Lake Road, Suite 100
Lincoln, NE 68512
www.iuniverse.com
1-800-Authors (1-800-288-4677)

ISBN-13: 978-0-595-39733-4 (pbk)
ISBN-13: 978-0-595-84139-4 (ebk)
ISBN-10: 0-595-39733-6 (pbk)
ISBN-10: 0-595-84139-2 (ebk)

Printed in the United States of America

Contents

ACKNOWLEDGEMENT. ix

INTRODUCTION xi

CHAPTER 1   ARE YOU READY FOR NEGOTIATIONS? . . . 1

- *Rule 1 Focus on the goal. Don't be distracted by your emotions.* *1*
- *Rule 2 Look forward, not back. The past is called the past for a reason.* *3*
- *Rule 3 You don't have to be right to settle.* *3*
- *Rule 4 Know what you want and what the other side wants* *4*
- *Rule 5 Be prepared and do your research* *5*
- *Rule 6 Get a reality check. What is it worth?* *6*
- *Rule 7 Always Have a Plan B.* *7*
- *Rule 8 Find out if the other side wants something other than money.* *8*

CHAPTER 2   NEGOTIATION STRATEGIES 10

- *Rule 9 Only Negotiate with Someone with Authority* *10*
- *Rule 10 Set the Tone and Look the Part.* *10*
- *Rule 11 Request Ground Rules* *11*
- *Rule 12 Volunteer and take control.* *12*
- *Rule 13 Agree on the issues and prioritize them.* *13*
- *Rule 14 Say What You Want.* *14*
- *Rule 15 You can negotiate with a lunatic* *14*
- *Rule 16 Be ethical and don't make promises you can't keep* *15*
- *Rule 17. Be willing to apologize.* *16*
- *Rule 18 Everyone makes mistakes* *16*
- *Rule 19 Never take or give no for an answer.* *17*
- *Rule 20 It doesn't hurt to ask. If you don't ask, you don't get.* *18*

- *Rule 21 Do not give anything away without getting something* *19*
- *Rule 22 Always ask for one more thing or be prepared to give one more thing* . *20*
- *Rule 23 know the rhythm of the negotiation* *20*
- *Rule 24 Keep track of the paperwork* *21*
- *Rule 25 Don't gloat* *22*
- *Rule 26 Beware and be aware* *22*
- *Rule 27 Tradeoff or Split the Difference* *23*
- *Rule 28 Do not negotiate against yourself* *23*
- *Rule 29 Be a devil's advocate* *24*
- *Rule 30 Save face* *24*
- *Rule 31 Watch the other side's body language* *25*

CHAPTER 3   EXTREME TACTICS 26
- *Rule 32 Have a Temper-Tantrum* *26*
- *Rule 33 Take Away or Walk Away* *27*
- *Rule 34 Do not overreach* *28*
- *Rule 35 Create a diversion such as a smoke screen, decoy or red herring* *29*
- *Rule 36 Take it or leave it.* *30*

CHAPTER 4   CLOSE THE DEAL 31
- *Rule 37 Step back and look at the big picture* *31*
- *Rule 38 The devil is in the details, but no detail is too insignificant if the other side wants it* *32*
- *Rule 39 Know when to close or when to fold.* *33*
- *Rule 40 Negotiation follow-up.* *34*
- *Rule 41 Do not expect thanks or gratitude when it is all over.* *35*

CHAPTER 5   OTHER FORMATS FOR NEGOTIATION. . . 36
- *A. How to Negotiate on the Telephone* *36*
- *B. How to Negotiate Online* *38*

CHAPTER 6   SPECIALIZED NEGOTIATIONS 42
- *A. How to Negotiate with your Boss* *43*
- *B. How to Negotiate with a Spouse or Ex-Spouse* *47*
- *C. How to Negotiate with a Hotel* *49*

- *D. How to negotiate on Ebay* *51*
  1) What is eBay and how does it work? 51
  2) What is feedback? 51
  3) How can negative feedback be withdrawn? 52

CHAPTER 7   WHAT HAPPENS WHEN NEGOTIATIONS FAIL? 58
- *Should you go to mediation?* *58*
- *Should you go to arbitration?* *59*
- *Should you go to Mediation/arbitration?* *59*
- *Where to file a complaint* *60*

APPENDIX A   GLOSSARY TERMS 63

APPENDIX B   WHAT MAKES A GOOD NEGOTIATOR? . . 69

APPENDIX C   DO'S AND DON'TS OF NEGOTIATORS . . . 71

APPENDIX D   GROUND RULES SAMPLE POLICY 75

It is not always someone's fault. There are situations where no one is to blame and there is no right or wrong side. Both sides assume the other has done something wrong; both sides believe the other person is lying and untrustworthy. Try to get beyond the immediate distrust and ask factual questions about the problem. Sometimes an innocent mistake has been made by one of the parties, who did not even realize it; sometimes the mistake was made by a third party. Parties that are concerned with what is right rather than settlement often don't want to compromise. If you want the negotiation to move forward, you may have to be the first one to give in or start the initiative or even accept some of the blame. If the other side is only interested in being right, chances are the situation won't be resolved.

Script:

I know that you think this is my fault, and maybe it is. How can we get beyond this blame game and move forward to a solution. What exactly do you want to resolve this?
You know, you are absolutely right. I made a big mistake. I want to apologize for that and hope you can forgive me. How would you like to proceed?
I don't think this was anyone's fault. I believe it was an honest mistake. Let's try to get to the bottom of this.
I wonder if this was sent to the right address or whether the address was correct. Tell me what your address is again so I can match it to the package.

RULE 4 KNOW WHAT YOU WANT AND WHAT THE OTHER SIDE WANTS

Knowing what you want may seem obvious, but many parties don't know what they want. They are so angry that they have not even asked themselves how the issue can be resolved. If they don't know what they want, how can they go about getting it? Instead they may want to hash and rehash the circumstances that got them into this negotiation.

Depending on the complexity of the situation, you should have a detailed plan of what you want. In addition to knowing what you want, you also need to know what you are willing to give up to get what you want. Generally you can get what you want if you are willing to pay the price for it. Don't ever begin a negotiation without knowing what you want.

Knowing what the other side wants is a little more difficult than knowing what you want. You cannot be certain if your assessment is accurate. How do you find out? Sometimes just asking the other side what they want will give you some idea. However, you may need to take their response with a grain of salt. You can look at previous negotiations if you have the records. In union negotiations, parties often ask for the same thing years after year. During the negotiation, you can look at body language. Sometimes the only way you can know is by making a counter-offer to something they offered you. Their acceptance of the counter-offer can give you some knowledge. You can also ask the other side to prioritize their issues. Sometimes the other side wants something that is not important to you. If you can find out what that something is, perhaps you can trade something for it. You may have a hunch about what the other side wants, but be sure to follow it up with facts and research.

Script

Can you tell me why you want this provision?
Can you make a counter-offer?
Can you prioritize these three issues so we know where to start
I have prepared a proposal and would like to circulate it and explain the details to you.

RULE 5 BE PREPARED AND DO YOUR RESEARCH

Once you have an idea what you want, you must do your research and preparation. That could be as simple as listing your arguments on a sheet of paper or as complex as doing the research to cost out a request for wage increases. Either way, you need to be prepared. Otherwise, you might make a concession (See Glossary) or agreement that you will later regret. You need to know the rationale behind your requests and a good estimate of the costs, including the future costs. If the negotiation is a complex one, you may want to consider an expert to do the number crunching for you.

In a negotiation, such as a union negotiation, much preliminary work needs to be done. When doing a proposal for wage increases, for example, internal information must be collected, such as number of employees, salaries, pay grade, as well as information from outside departments in other cities in the county and neighboring counties that are comparable. When you collect statistics, you need to see if they are prepared the same way you are preparing your comparable numbers. It is very important that the statistics you report are accurate and the underlying rationale understood. The statistics should also be in a format that is easily understood and explained.

Nothing is more embarrassing than making a presentation and having someone question the accuracy of your numbers and having the whole presentation fall apart because the data is confusing, or even worse incorrect. Sometimes the other side will have their own set of data. If you can get the other side to agree with your data, it will make the negotiations run more smoothly. Even if the other side does not agree on your numbers, it will still be helpful if the other side can agree on the methodology or format. It may take more effort on your side, but it is always an advantage to work from your statistics or your drafts, especially if the other side signs off on them.

If you are not completely prepared, consider delaying the start of the negotiation. If you go in with little or no information, and try to wing it, you will regret it later. You cannot be over-prepared. Even if you don't use everything you prepared, it does not matter. It is important to have as much information and research as possible just in case you need it. Of course, when something unforeseen comes up at the negotiating table, you can ask for time to research, but that can break the rhythm. The more you do in advance, the easier the negotiations will be. You should also expect the other side to be prepared. When they make a proposal, you need to question how they arrived at their numbers.

Script

Here is my first proposal and I wanted to tell you why this is so important and how much this will cost this year and in future years.
I have viewed your proposal. I am a little confused how you arrived at your numbers. I would like to know the process and rationale you used.
We are having our finance department work up some numbers. If both parties can agree on the methodology or format, then it will be a lot easier to negotiate pay increases.

RULE 6 GET A REALITY CHECK. WHAT IS IT WORTH?

If a dispute is to be resolved, the parties have to be realistic. When the party asks for something outrageous or unreasonable, there has to be a reality check. If you have done adequate preparation and research, you should be able to rebut a request that is not rational. Some parties start with totally exaggerated proposals just so they can give something later on. You might use your sense of humor to convey that you are willing to be reasonable but that what they are asking for is totally out of the question

Whether it is a car, a raise at work, a house, a pedigreed dog or a collectible on eBay, you need to know what it is worth before you start the negotiation. You also need to set a spending or buying limit before you begin the negotiation. If you are buying or selling something, you need to do some comparative shopping. A good source is the internet, especially eBay. Looking at selling prices for comparable items can be a good reality check. What an item is worth is often a lot less than what you paid for it and less than a listing in a catalogue unless the item is extremely rare. Be sure to get the right comparables. For example the value of a coin can be affected by the date, condition or mintage. It is important to know the item's rarity. If something is readily available, buyers might not offer much because they know that if they don't get the item from you, they can get it somewhere else. However, if your item is very rare, then the whole psychology is different. Now the buys know that if they don't buy it from you, there probably won't be another chance anytime soon.

Script

Seller: The price of this item on eBay is 40 % less than the catalogue. I have to make a profit, too.
Buyer: I have done a lot of research on this item and because of its rarity, it is worth $500. This exact one sold for $600 on eBay.
I have read your proposal and if we were to take it seriously, you have requested an increase of 500%.
You only paid $25 and now you want $250 for your time and. aggravation My time is valuable, too, but I am not going to charge you for that either.

RULE 7 ALWAYS HAVE A PLAN B

It is an important strategy to always have a backup plan. As they say, you should not put all your eggs in one basket. You should be asking yourself questions that start with *how* or what *if*? How can I sweeten the deal? How can I close the deal? What if the party likes this? What if they reject this? Try to come up with some alternatives that will help seal the deal. Having a Plan B gets easier the more you negotiate. It becomes a way to be flexible and react to what the other side wants and think fast on your feet.

Script

If you don't like that one, here is a beauty. Why don't you take it home and show your wife.
I can give you a package deal. If you take this one, I will throw this one in for free.

RULE 8 FIND OUT IF THE OTHER SIDE WANTS SOMETHING OTHER THAN MONEY.

Sometimes the other party wants something other than money such as time or an apology. We are so used to negotiating about money that sometimes we forget that money is not everything. For example a truly heartfelt apology can go a long way to help resolve a consumer dispute. If the other side feels that the apology is sincere, the apology may even be enough to close the deal. An employee might want time-off instead of money. You may be able to suggest part-time work or flex time or vacation time if the employee is one that you want to keep. Sometimes what is wanted is convenience rather than money. The employees want a day care center and are willing to pay for it. These suggestions may be a way to resolve the problem and to save money at the same time. Sometimes you can work on a policy together that can be implemented. This way both parties buy into the process and the final product. Be careful that there are not hidden costs. For example a day care facility may have liability issues that you have not factored into the cost.

Sometimes the other side wants something that is not important to you. If you can find out what that something is, it is a painless way of resolving a dispute. For example an employee might want a raise and a new title. If you can agree on a title that reflects the person's duties, but you don't have enough money for a raise, that might be a way to give an employee something that she wants. She might be willing to wait six months or a year for the raise if she gets the title right away. If you can keep what is important to you but make a concession that is not important to you, that is good negotiations.

Script:

We have very limited resources. However, if we work together on the flexible time policy and it makes employees more productive, we would be more likely to approve it.
What is your first priority? We have limited resources, but if it is important to you, we may be able to work something out.
I can make that new title effective today, but you would have to wait six months for the raise.

2

NEGOTIATION STRATEGIES

Now that you have done your preparations and research, you are now ready to review the strategies that you can use in Negotiations.

RULE 9 ONLY NEGOTIATE WITH SOMEONE WITH AUTHORITY

Someone with authority (See Glossary) is someone who can speak or act on behalf of the company or employer. If you are not dealing with someone with authority, then you are not really negotiating and are wasting your time. If you are not sure whether a person has authority to give you what you want, ask them directly. If you are in a more complex setting, you may ask for a written statement from the principal that this agent speaks or acts on his behalf. Sometimes someone will have the authority to act on someone else's behalf, but they may have restrictions such as a set monetary amount. They can sell you an item at a certain price but cannot go any lower. This is important because you do not want to find out at the very end that the person you thought you were negotiating with did not have any the authority to do so.

Script

Before we begin, I want to make sure that you have the authority to negotiate on this matter.

RULE 10 SET THE TONE AND LOOK THE PART

You are the one who should set the tone of the negotiation. When you come into the room for the first time, you should look the part. You should wear professional clothes. If a woman, don't wear a lot of distracting jewelry. Act as though you know what you are doing and get to business quickly. Have a notebook and a briefcase and start right in. Project the image that you want to project. You might even try it in the mirror a few times. You want to give good eye contact and be a good listener. You want to seem knowledgeable about the issue or issues to be discussed. You can state what your philosophy is and what your negotiation style is. Think of the qualities of a negotiator that you admire most and try to project them. For example, my idea of a good negotiator is someone who is firm, flexible, fair, and honest, and has a good sense of humor. That is the tone I would like to set.

Script

My approach to negotiation is based on trust and my style is based on fairness.

RULE 11 REQUEST GROUND RULES

At the first session, the procedural aspects of the negotiations should be discussed. Ask for the parties to agree to ground rules. A negotiation goes more smoothly if ground rules are adopted. Then if something goes awry, one can point out the ground rule that has been violated. See the Glossary Appendix D for a sample Ground Rules Policy.

The ground rules should set out the time and place for the negotiations. Rules concerning the procedures for each day are very important and will save you time in the long run. For example, you can set out a timetable for the parties to follow. The agenda for the next meeting will be prepared at the previous meeting; the proposals will be distributed at the second meeting; or the topics to be negotiated will be selected at the fourth meeting. Who can call a caucus?

The role of the spokesperson needs to be spelled out. Is the spokesperson the only one allowed to negotiate or to accept or reject proposals or counter-proposals? Rules of conduct need to be addressed. Only one person will speak at any time and will not be interrupted. Everyone will speak with courtesy and there will be no profanity. Both parties agree to comply with reasonable requests for information and pay reasonable reproduction costs. There can be special rules on the use of cell phones, including where and when they are prohibited and whether they should be shut off.

If there is a negotiating team, there would be internal rules to follow. If a team member wants to speak, he writes a note to the spokesperson to call a caucus. Negotiation materials will be kept secure. The negotiations are confidential and are not to be discussed outside the team. Each team member will have an assignment and will attend all sessions.

Using the ground rules on the first session really helps set the tone for the negotiation. Everyone knows what is expected and the negotiations become more professional.

Script

Let's see if we can agree to a set of ground rules, If you like, I can draft a sample and we can see which ones we can use.

RULE 12 VOLUNTEER AND TAKE CONTROL

You want to get as much control of the negotiation that you can. One way you can do this is to volunteer anytime you can during the negotiation. Volunteer to prepare the agenda; volunteer to draft ground rules (see Rule 11 above); volunteer to type up the day's notes; volunteer to get comparables numbers from the internet; volunteer to prioritize the issues; volunteer to frame the issue; and volunteer to give an opening statement first. Volunteer, volunteer, volunteer!

Preparing the agenda is a tactical advantage because you can determine who goes first and make some preliminary suggestions as to the order and priority of negotiation topics. Being in charge of the note—taking is also an advantage as long as it is done accurately and in a timely fashion. First of all it helps keep you organized by having someone take notes and make drafts. Using your computer and your software makes it less likely that a mistake is made as to the final language in the finished product.

If the other side is strapped for time or does not want to take on the responsibility of these projects, your offer may be accepted. Although volunteering may mean extra work, it will usually pay off in the long run. Volunteering is a way for you to control the negotiation and to get your opinions and solutions out front. Of course, if you are volunteering for a project such as doing the agenda or preparing notes, be sure that you spend enough time on this and don't make mistakes. If you do sloppy work, then volunteering is not going to be an advantage. It could be a real detriment if you start confusing yourself and the other side.

Script

I am willing to type up the day's notes and circulate them.
If you want, I can prepare the agenda for each meeting

RULE 13 AGREE ON THE ISSUES AND PRIORITIZE THEM.

If both parties can agree on the issue or issues at the first session or second session, this saves time and effort. As noted above in Rule 12, Volunteer and Take Control, it is usually an advantage for you to state what the issue is. The other party can react to it and either agree or disagree with your statement. Hopefully both parties can fine tune the issue or issues so both parties can agree. If it is a fairly complex issue, it helps to reduce the issue or issues to writing so that both parties can agree in writing. This helps move the negotiations forward, but it can also be helpful to document what the issues were if challenged later.

If there is more than one issue, it is important to prioritize them. You should determine this for yourself, but you may not want to divulge this to the other side right away. If you can get the other side to tell you what their priorities are, this will help your strategy. You can probably guess what the other side's priorities are, but you may be surprised.

Once you know your issues and their priority, then you need to decide which ones to negotiate first. Some negotiators like to start with the easy issues to gain some momentum and then move on into the more complicated items. Other negotiators like to start with a complex issue. When that gets resolved, the less important issues fall into place to complete the negotiation. You will have to make your own decision on this. If this is your first negotiation or you are not sure, it is better to start with the easy items. It develops mutual trust and respect that can carry on through the rest of the negotiation and it helps set the tone for the rest of the sessions. You can get bogged down very early in the negotiation if you begin with a complex issue.

Script

If we can agree to the issue we are trying to resolve, that should point us in the right direction for resolution.
Let's see if can agree on some of the smaller issues before we move on to the more complex issues.

Let's start with the most difficult issue. Once that is resolved, it will be smooth sailing to resolve the other issues.

RULE 14 SAY WHAT YOU WANT.

This is a little different from knowing what you want. Even if you know what you want, you still have to articulate it properly. You need to determine how you are going to present what you want and the rationale behind it. In your first request, you generally need to ask for more than what you want so you can leave room for some bargaining room and compromise. This can be tricky. If you ask for too much, you might not be taken seriously. If you don't ask for enough, you may end up compromising and getting less than you anticipated. Don't hem and haw and be indecisive. Be clear as to what your position is.

Script

I have one major goal in this negotiation and this is it:

RULE 15 YOU CAN NEGOTIATE WITH A LUNATIC

Even if the other side is crazy, it is possible to get a settlement. The best way to respond to someone who says something totally absurd or ridiculous is to ignore it. It may be logical to him in some way. Usually I won't tell the person how ridiculous their claim or counter-offer is because that may offend him. I try to point out what I am willing to pay and ask if there is anything else he wants such as an apology or another item.

Sometimes I use humor to try to deflect his frustration, but this can sometimes back fire and make him madder. If the person insists on his outrageous position, we may reach an impasse or deadlock. It seems fairly obvious that he is playing a game and has no intent of resolving the dispute. I will try to get him to discuss it logically, but this usually does not work. These are the hardest cases to resolve because the other person often prefers to rant and rave rather than work on settling their issue

Script:

I am trying to understand what you really want. You are asking me for something I cannot do. I cannot pay you three times what the bid was. I may be able to send you something else from my catalogue at no cost and no extra shipping. Maybe you can make a realistic counter offer.
I think you are joking, right? Tell me what you really want.

RULE 16 BE ETHICAL AND DON'T MAKE PROMISES YOU CAN'T KEEP

When you are setting the tone for the negotiation, you want to be known as fair and honest. As a negotiator, you should not compromise your ethics. Whether you are a professional negotiator or negotiating within your family or at work, it is always important to keep your reputation intact. If you are thinking of doing or saying something and you are not sure whether it is unethical or not, I use this model. I ask myself whether my mother would approve or how I would feel if this situation were a headline in the local newspaper. If your mother would not approve or you would not like to see that headline in the local paper, then don't do or say it. It is always better to err on the side of being ethical or honest. Even if something has the appearance of being unethical, don't do that either. Remember that once something happens to your reputation or credibility, it is very difficult, if almost impossible, to get it back.

It is very important not to promise something and later change your mind. Whether it is intentional or unintentional, it is still unacceptable. Promising something that you know you cannot deliver is dishonest and unethical. Usually this happens when one side gets caught up in the moment and blurts out something. Sometimes the negotiator does not have the authority to give something and agrees to something that the higher authority later vetoes. Be very careful about agreeing to anything. As they say, if it sounds too good to be true, it probably is. It is much less embarrassing to take a break and call your higher authority to see if he/she agrees or to wait until the next day to be able to study the proposal more carefully.

Sometimes at the end of a negotiation, momentum develops so both sides want to resolve all issues and it is easy to agree to something you will later regret. Be sure the first time. However, mistakes do happen and if you know that you cannot keep your promise, break the news as soon as possible to the other side and apologize and try to move on with the negotiation.

Script

My reputation is important to me and I am not going to do anything that would tarnish it.
I just discovered that I approved something I now know was a mistake. I am very sorry, but we will need to renegotiate this provision. I am very sorry for the inconvenience this has caused.

RULE17. BE WILLING TO APOLOGIZE

Sometimes one party only wants an apology and the other side is too stubborn to give one. One side can get very childish and say, "It is against my principles" or "He has to apologize first" or "I did not do anything that warrants an apology". Even if you believe the other side is wrong, being willing to apologize can make often resolve the dispute. If the apology gets stuck in your craw, you can phrase it so you don't violate your "*principles*". A sincere apology, and I mean sincere, can go a long way. It can be very satisfying to the other side because we always want to be right If an apology can resolve a dispute or even help resolve a dispute, I consider it a cheap way to get what I want. If you use the right approach and keep your eye on the goal of resolving the situation, the apology will not be that painful. Swallow your pride and apologize.

Script:

I am sorry that I upset you
I am sorry that we had a communication problem
I am really sorry that I lost my temper.

RULE 18 EVERYONE MAKES MISTAKES

Things happen and mistakes are inevitable. There are two sides to making mistakes. If you find that you made a mistake such as sending the wrong item to a customer or did not include everything in the package, it is much better to "fess" up as soon as possible. It is better for you to tell them; if they find out for themselves, they will assume you did it on purpose.

If you are on the receiving end of a mistake, this is a chance to be magnanimous and understanding. Mistakes are inevitable. Always remember that the goal is to resolve the dispute. The sooner you put the mistake behind you, the sooner you can concentrate on the solution. Don't make the solution overly complicated or get too many people involved in it. If you sent the wrong item to the wrong person, don't expect them to send it back to a third party. It might be better to offer a refund at this point.

If it is not known who made the mistake, a lot of wasted effort can be directed at the events that led up to the mistake. Try to get back into the present and concentrate on a solution not who is at fault.

Script:

(You made the mistake) I was reviewing our tentative agreement last night and realized that I agreed to something in error. I apologize for the error; it is entirely my fault and I will have to take that off the table.
(The other party made the mistake) Thanks for admitting that you made an error. We all make mistakes and let's see how we can move forward to resolve this.
(A mistake has been made but no one will admit it). Mistakes happen. Let's not dwell on who made the mistake, but let's concentrate on how we might go about correcting and resolving this.

RULE 19 NEVER TAKE OR GIVE NO FOR AN ANSWER.

If you ask for something you really want and it is denied, don't take no for an answer. Try to find out why they are saying "no". As they say, there is more than one way to skin a cat. Try to think of a different way to convince the other side to give you what you want. Go back to the drawing board and try to ask for what you want in a different way. Even a minor change, a compromise or rephrasing might make it more palatable. If this is an important issue, suggest a trade-off or package deal, so the other side might be motivated by getting something they want.

If you really want to resolve something, giving "no" as an answer does not help the negotiation. However, if you must say "no", temper its effect so that it seems that you are willing to compromise or give some hope of a concession. Try to offer a scaled-down version of the original request if you have some leeway. If you absolutely must say" no" to the proposal, explain why you cannot go forward on this issue and temper the impact with positive discussion on other issues. If you know this is an important issue for the other side, listen to their arguments very carefully so you can determine if their arguments would allow you to change your mind. Don't give up. You may be able to get something you really want in exchange.

Script

This is an extensive proposal which we could not institute in one year. Why don't you come back with a scaled down version that can be done in the next fiscal year?

I have reviewed your proposal. We could not agree to A, but I see some promise in B. Why don't you tell me what you are trying to accomplish in B and maybe we can work something out.

I understand what you are saying, but what if we did it this way?

I am not sure why you are so opposed to this. Can you explain it to me?

I could give you this if you give me that.

RULE 20 IT DOESN'T HURT TO ASK. IF YOU DON'T ASK, YOU DON'T GET.

It does not hurt to ask for something. The worse that can happen is that the other person says no. This is true in any kind of negotiation, especially in dealing with your boss. Ask for that raise or promotion from your boss. Even if you don't get it, he/she may admire your pluck and keep you in mind for future promotions. If there is something very important to you, it is good to get it out on the table. However, do your research and be prepared to defend what it is you want and why you should get it. Don't think that if you deserve a raise or promotion, you will get it without initiating the conversation. If you have a bad customer service experience at a hotel, ask for something like an upgrade or a free night's stay. You may be surprised and get it. The other side is not going to give you what you want unless you tell them what it is you want.

Script

I know it is not promotion review time yet, but since you told me what a great job I did on that project you gave me last month, I think that a raise would reward me for my hard work.

I have done a lot of research and I am the lowest paid department head in the city even though I have the most longevity. I would like you to review my research and consider bringing my salary up to $80,000, which is the median salary for department heads.

RULE 21 DO NOT GIVE ANYTHING AWAY WITHOUT GETTING SOMETHING

This is a simple rule but often violated. Sometimes it is tempting, especially at the beginning of the negotiation, to offer something to the other side to show how magnanimous you are. But the result is really giving away something for nothing and sets a bad precedent for you. You have your bargaining chips (See Glossary) and you should get something for each one. Of course, if you can get something without even giving up something, that is even better.

Bargaining chips are something that can be offered to the other side in order to get something from the other side. It is important not to use these up in the beginning of the negotiation. It can be tempting to be generous and give up most of your chips in the beginning of the negotiation. However, you need to have some bargaining chips in reserve to help finalize the negotiations. You always want to end the negotiation with a few extra chips in reserve, not the other way round. The expression bargaining chip comes from the poker table and you need to negotiate like a poker player with a poker face so the other side does not know what is "left in your cards."

Script

I cannot give you something unless you give me something back
I really don't have much else to give. I am tapped out. However, if we can finalize the negotiations today, I might be able to find some money for that project.

RULE 22 ALWAYS ASK FOR ONE MORE THING OR BE PREPARED TO GIVE ONE MORE THING

There are some people in a negotiation who are never going to be satisfied. Just when you think you have an agreement, they want one more thing. This is human nature, I guess, to squeeze as much out of the other side as possible. Knowing this trait will allow you to always keep a bargaining chip (see Glossary) or two up your sleeve for this contingency when you are trying to wrap up negotiations. When someone wants one last thing, perhaps you can get one last thing as well.

The flip side is the same. If you are in a negotiation that is almost completed, the excitement rises as the last few issues are getting resolved. Always have a last minute request to get another item into the agreement. Don't overuse this strategy because you may find you don't have an agreement because the parties cannot agree on this last *one more thing*.

Parties are more likely to agree to these last minute requests if they think it will finally resolve the dispute. However, it can backfire, if the other side is offended that something new is being brought up at such a late time. Use judiciously. Remember there are some people who always have to have the last word. Use this trait to your advantage.

Script:

If you can agree to this one last thing, I think we have an agreement.
If you give me my last request, I can agree to your last request and we have a deal.
When will this ever end? I thought we already had an agreement and I am offended that you come back today asking for something else. I just cannot agree. You have gone too far!
Since you agree with that, let's go on to the next article

RULE 23 KNOW THE RHYTHM OF THE NEGOTIATION

The tempo of a dispute resolution is very important. Even knowing someone's personality can be helpful. You need to read the other party and know how to deal with them. If you know the preferred tempo of the other side, you can use that to help resolve the case. Some parties want to go over every little detail and don't care if the session lasts all day or night. Others want to look only at the big picture and want to spend as little time on the details as possible. This knowledge can work to your advantage especially when the tempo picks up at the end.

Sometimes, you may be surprised that the other side agreed to something you wanted. If this happens, consider yourself fortunate and move on to the next item. Don't over—analyze their agreement; act as though you were expecting it. The worst thing you can do is question it and say something like, "Are sure you agree with the whole section?" Keep the momentum going and consider yourself lucky

You will need to pick up the tempo if you are dealing with someone who can't make decisions and loves details. The negotiation takes on a rhythm of its own and you should respect that tempo. Don't rush it but don't let it get too long. Sometimes there are reasons that the other side does not want the negotiation to end. For example, an employee might not want to go back to his regular job and hopes to string out the negotiation sessions as long as possible since this is their free pass from work. You need to be aware of this tempo and adjust it when necessary.

Script:

Now that we have built a foundation and agreed on some major provisions, I think we can pick up the pace. Do you agree?
We have really made some progress. However, I think we may be going a little too fast. I would like to sleep on it and come back refreshed tomorrow.

RULE 24 KEEP TRACK OF THE PAPERWORK

In a complex negotiation, it is very important to keep track of what has been approved. One way to handle this is to have one person keep notes and print the notes after each meeting. It is very important to number the drafts or put a date on each one so you know which version you are reviewing. If you are negotiating alone, it is very difficult to take notes when you are talking and react to what is being said all at the same time. However, you should try to write up what happened each day after the session so you can keep track of what has happened.

If you start getting confused, mistakes will be made and it will be a sign of weakness. Having the correct information is always a sign of strength. If you can provide the correct date, time and content of previous discussions when there is disagreement, you will be in control and have the advantage.

Script

I went back into my notes and found we already approved that section on April 10.
We did not agree on that section yet. My notes say that we postponed that decision until we could get more information as to the cost.

RULE 25 DON'T GLOAT

If the negotiations seem to be going your way and you are getting what you want, don't gloat or smirk. This can infuriate the other side. You should have a poker face so no one can tell whether you are happy or frustrated or how the negotiations are going. You may have to work on this because it is human nature to show a little emotion when things are going well. If the other side thinks you are gloating, they will know that you are happy about something that they gave away. They will really be on their guard and the negotiations may even turn the other way. If you gloat, the other side will want to get something so they can gloat, too.

Script

I am not smirking. The sun is in my eyes
I was just laughing at a joke someone told me this morning.

RULE 26 BEWARE AND BE AWARE

Be aware and do not let your guard down. Even if you think the negotiations are going well, don't be lulled into complacency. Always be alert and vigilant and make sure you understand the ramifications of any agreement. The poker game analogy works here as well. If you keep your poker face, it will be hard for the other side to interpret your moves. However, if you are tired or frustrated at the end of the day, you may sigh or let your face show how discouraged you really are.

Be careful what you say and how you say it. Everything you say should be planned and part of your overall strategy. How you say it is also very important. Don't say anything off the cuff. It is also important not to be too cocky or too confident or, on the other extreme, too hesitant or informal. Being patronizing can also be annoying to the other side. Usually it is best to have a neutral demeanor and occasionally use some emotion to show what is really important to you or to throw the other side off. It is all in the delivery.

Script

Don't let this demeanor fool you. I am paying attention
I don't like to show my hand, but this item is very important to me.

RULE 27 TRADEOFF OR SPLIT THE DIFFERENCE

A tradeoff is sometimes called *Quid Pro Quo*, which is Latin for this for that. It means that if you give me what I want, I will give you what you want. We use the tradeoff in every day negotiating. It is natural to say that if you give me this, I will give you that. It seems fair and it is a way to compromise without giving up that much because you are getting something back in return. If you can trade something you don't even want, that is even better

Splitting the difference is a good strategy to use especially near the end of negotiations. If you feel some momentum and the parties are weary, that is the perfect time to suggest that since you are so close on a particular point, why don't you just split the difference? This won't work if you are very far apart. It can work if you are willing to give in a little to finish the negotiation on a particular provision or complete negotiations altogether.

Script:

I am wiling to do a trade off. If we go to the Japanese restaurant this week, we can go to the Mexican restaurant next week.
We are so close on this dollar amount. Why don't we just split the difference and call it a day?

RULE 28 DO NOT NEGOTIATE AGAINST YOURSELF

When you negotiate against yourself you are asked to bid against yourself. For example if you make an offer of $10,000 and the other side does not answer or give a counter offer, and then you offer $15,000, you are bidding or negotiating against yourself. When you are in a hurry, it is easy to do. You get some indication that your offer is not high enough and you start escalating the offers. However, it is always better to ask for a counter offer. Make the other side do some work. If you are negotiating against yourself, you may actually offer something higher than what the other side was willing to accept.

Script

I feel as though I am negotiating against my self. I cannot make you another offer until you make me a counter-offer.

RULE 29 BE A DEVIL'S ADVOCATE

Being a devil's advocate (See Glossary) is a way to give a reality check to the other side and point out the flaws in their side's arguments or the downside of their proposals. By saying you are going to play the devil's advocate, you are not your own advocate. It is a convention so it does not appear that you are actually making the comments on your own behalf. By taking on the outsider's role, you can point out the flaws in the other side's case. It is a great device or foil because the other side cannot take offense. It is not you talking; it is the devil.

Script

Let me play devil's advocate for a minute. If we were to agree to that, it would cost us 10 times what we are paying now.

RULE 30 SAVE FACE

Saving face is a way to allow someone to get out of an embarrassing or problem situation with their dignity intact. Sometimes people are afraid to admit they are wrong. The other side can help them save face by giving a way out. This is the opposite of driving someone into a corner, which will make a person fight even harder. Giving some one a way out is a tradition in many countries. This can work in negotiations because it is a way to help the other side avoid embarrassment. It is often used in politics. Something is done so the President can save face and not be embarrassed. You are helping the other side not look bad and, as a result, may get some concessions.

It is also a way to be creative about a solution. For example if you have a high-ranking employee who is not performing his job for some reason, you may want to demote him. This could be devastating to the employee's ego, so perhaps he gets a lateral transfer and a different title so he can go into the other position with dignity and not be humiliated. In such a situation, the employee may be a better worker rather than be angry and mad about a demotion. Don't expect too much if you help someone save face.

Script

If we allow that employee to retire, he might be able to save face.

RULE 31 WATCH THE OTHER SIDE'S BODY LANGUAGE

Watching the other person's body language can tell you a lot about them. If someone is avoiding eye contact, he or she might be lying or unsure of something. If the other side has outbursts and is angry, he or she might be trying to ambush you or take control of the situation. You have to determine whether this is staged or for real. If for real, the other side might let their emotions get the best of him. If a person's head is in their hand, they might be frustrated or tired. If their hands are folded, that is a sign of a closed position; arms out show an open position. Stroking one's face usually means a person is thinking or planning the next move. If the other side is friendly, that usually means confidence.

If the other side is indifferent or hesitates, it could be a sign of weakness. Be careful not to put too much stock into body language. The other side may be acting and trying to throw you off. However, some expressions are reflexive and people don't have that much control. Remember, the other side might be looking at you to determine your state of mind. Negotiation is a lot like the game of poker. Having a poker face—that is a neutral expression that does not show whether you have good or bad cards—is the best appraoch.

Script

When he does not look me in the eye, I think he is lying

3

EXTREME TACTICS

This chapter lists a few tactics which I normally would not use in negotiations unless it was going very poorly and I was willing to pull out all the stops. If you are dealing with a person with whom you have had previous favorable negotiations, you probably don't want to use these tactics. If you are dealing with a person with whom you expect to have future negotiations, then don't use these tactics either. Be cautious before using any of them and be aware that they can backfire. If you are at a point where things could not get any worse and you are ready to give up altogether, you might want to consider one or two of them. Use them sparingly. I am also including these extreme tactics so that you will recognize them if the other side uses them against you.

RULE 32 HAVE A TEMPER-TANTRUM

If you want to make a point, a deliberately staged temper tantrum might fit the bill. What makes this effective is that is unexpected. If done sparingly, you can show that you mean business and are not to be messed with. It can also backfire. If the negotiation is particularly volatile anyway and the parties are already discourteous and rude, a temper tantrum is not going to stand out. If you do get angry, it should be on purpose and staged for effect. This should be done very sparingly, if at all, like an actor in a play. Generally it is better to be polite and charming, but not too charming or you will appear to be insincere. If you get angry and it is not staged, then you will be out of control. As Shakespeare said in *As You Like It*, "All the world is a stage and all the men and women merely players." The whole negotiation process is acting to some degree. You do not want the other side to know what your position is and how you really feel. However, on rare occasions, you may feel that the timing is right to show anger. Just make sure you are really acting and that you are in control.

When you are on your last nerve and you are told your reserved hotel room has been given to someone else, that controlled anger may be a way to get the hotel's attention since they would want you to stop making a scene. On the other hand, you are always taking a chance that you will humiliate yourself. It is best to do this when you have nothing to lose and may never see this person again. Calculate beforehand whether the planned outburst is worth the risks. If you go forward, prepare your script and practice just as an actor would do. Give details so the person knows why you are so upset. Remember it is to be controlled so don't go overboard with your performance. If you turn red in the face and start perspiring, your performance might have gone too far. When you do stage a scene like this, always end with a proposed solution. Otherwise your performance may be wasted and the other party may not feel like proposing a solution after you have yelled at them.

Script

I have really had it to here! You want to know why I am mad! I am going to tell you!
I am really mad about this and I am not going to take it any more! I cannot believe that you would even suggest such a thing

RULE 33 TAKE AWAY OR WALK AWAY

This tactic is threatening to take away something that is already part of a previous agreement even though you will probably give it back. This creates the illusion of giving something to the other side, but the reality is that it probably won't be taken away. The idea is to make the other side give up something else in order to retain the benefit. You need to be aware of this technique if someone tries to use it against you. However, there may be situations where one party determines that a previous benefit is too expensive and wants to revise and remove it.

Sometimes you may feel that if you don't get what you want, you are ready to walk away. If you use this tactic in the negotiation process, use it sparingly. For example, if you want to make a point about the other side's behavior or tactics, you may want to say something strong and leave the room. Remember, if you do get mad (See Rule 32, Have a Temper Tantrum, above), that it should be staged. You don't want to really lose control. If you fly off the handle every time something goes wrong, you will be crying wolf and the tactic will be ignored.

For example you might decide that you are going to ask for a raise or a promotion and you are prepared to quit if you don't get it. Be careful when making this kind of gesture. You don't want to quit your job just because you lost your temper. You may want to resist that urge to go into your boss's office and go home and sleep on it. There are other ways to negotiate a raise which don't have the dire consequences of losing your job. On the other hand if you have a good job offer and you are testing the waters to see if you can get an increase and stay at your current job, that is a different story.

If someone came to me when I was a Director of Human Resources and threatened to quit, I would often put a piece of paper in front of him and ask him to write, "I resign" and sign and date it before he changed his mind. Usually I had already pegged that employee as a problem employee. If I wanted to keep the employee, I might want to try to work something out. This is an extreme tactic and only use if you are really ready to walk. Don't bluff if you are not prepared to take the consequences. Don't say you are gong to quit if you are not willing to follow through. You will lose any negotiating power you have if you come back the next day begging for your job back.

Script

We negotiated this all last time; I am not sure why we are going through this again.
We gave up flexible time last year so we could have increased health insurance. If you want to revisit this, we need to get our flexible time back.
You are not giving me much choice. If I must choose between giving you a promotion and you leaving the firm, I will have to choose that you leave. We don't have any vacant positions now.
You are a good employee and I don't want to see you leave. Why don't you come back tomorrow so you can tell me why you think you deserve a raise.

RULE 34 DO NOT OVERREACH

If you overreach and use ruthless tactics such as an ambush to annihilate the other side in a negotiation, the other side will want to retaliate at the next negotiation or even sooner. You may have won the battle but lost the war. You may have gotten some concessions for your side, but the relationship with the other side is now completely deteriorated and full of distrust. You want to get as much as you can in a negotiation, but there will be consequences if you go to extremes.

If the other side is beaten down and so humiliated that they look bad to their members, they will be looking for an opportunity to humiliate you. The consequences of overreaching might not be immediately apparent, but the other side will wait for the right moment to avenge their humiliation.

If you are the one who overreached, you might not want to wait for retaliation and meet with the other side and repair some of the damage of the negotiations. It is difficult to have a good working relationship after negotiations have gone bad.

Script

We don't trust you anymore or believe anything you say after you used your dirty tricks in the last negotiations.
I thought the negotiation was going well until we were ambushed. We were not expecting that. We will expect it next time though

RULE 35 CREATE A DIVERSION SUCH AS A SMOKE SCREEN, DECOY OR RED HERRING

In the military setting, smoke is released to mask the location or moving of troops. In the negotiation setting, it is a way to mask your true intent or mask what is important. A smoke screen is a diversionary tactic to take attention away from your main objective and give attention to something of little or no importance. This can backfire if the other side realizes you are just wasting their time.

A decoy or red herring (See Glossary) is a tactic to mislead the other party and create a diversion. Of course, the origin of the *decoy* is duck hunting, but the origin of the term red herring is more obscure. Red herring was rubbed on hounds to protect the hunted fox or fugitives from being caught. The hounds will smell the herring rather than the scent of the fox or men. A red herring is essentially a false clue or phony issue that is used to distract the voters or negotiators from the real issues.

We know that the issue of seniority is just a smoke screen. You are really wasting our time. Let's get back to something that is important.
All that discussion about safety was just a red herring. I know what the real issue is.

RULE 36 TAKE IT OR LEAVE IT

The take it or leave it approach was used in a famous labor case in the 1950's involving Lemuel Boulware, a vice-president for General Electric. Mr. Boulware went through a process of determining what was best for the company and what it could afford and presented his first, last and best offer as a package deal to the electrical union and basically said, "Take it or leave it". The Court determined that this was not good faith bargaining because there was no give or take between the parties and no involvement by the union. This take it or leave it approach is now called Boulwareism (sometimes spelled Boulwarism), named after that General Electric vice-president who first used it. This approach is not really negotiation since both sides are not involved. One side is saying, this is what we want (or are willing to give) and we won't take (or give) anything less.

This technique should not be used in a negotiation today, especially at the start of negotiations. However, if you are at the end of a negotiation, it might be an approach to use if phrased correctly. Never say that something is your final offer unless you have nothing else to give and you are already very near the end of the negotiations. Saying it this way is not an unfair labor practice since the parties have been involved in the give and take of negotiations. Never say this is the final offer unless you really mean it and are willing to walk away

Script

If you are saying, take it or leave it, we will leave it.
This is not Boulwareism. We want to hear your reaction to our proposal.

4

CLOSE THE DEAL

After you have been negotiating for a long time, it can get frustrating and tiring when the negotiations go on and on and nothing seems to be happening or get resolved. Sometimes the negotiations even start to unravel. Here are some rules to help complete the negotiations.

RULE 37 STEP BACK AND LOOK AT THE BIG PICTURE

During dispute resolution, we are looking at the small picture. We are dealing with the facts and details of a dispute that is important to the parties but is not earth-shattering to anyone else. It is important to step back once in a while and see where the dispute is in the big picture of your life, world events, etc. Some people can get really wrapped up in whether the dispute is resolved and have a lot of frustration and anger, sometimes over trivia. When weighed against world peace or world events, it just loses its significance. If the case is not resolved at all or you feel that you gave up more than you wanted, it does help to step back and look at the big picture. Sometimes doing this makes you take yourself less seriously. The other benefit is that sometimes you realize that this is the time to throw in the towel and close the negotiations.

Script.

You know I have worked long and hard on this negotiation. However, if we don't resolve it, it won't be the end of the world. Let's try one more time to see if we can resolve it and if we can't, let's call it quits.

RULE 38 THE DEVIL IS IN THE DETAILS, BUT NO DETAIL IS TOO INSIGNIFICANT IF THE OTHER SIDE WANTS IT

Even when there is preliminary agreement, be sure that all loose ends are tied down. Try to anticipate any contingency so that negotiations don't break down at a later time. It is easy in the excitement of resolving a long and complex dispute to stop the negotiations when there seems to be initial agreement and put off writing down the details. If you are too tired to continue, at least prepare a draft with all the details to bring to the next meeting. That initial excitement can get deflated when the parties come back the next day and say that the written document does not reflect their agreement. If you are caught in this situation, try to force yourself to write it down in a clear and accurate statement of the agreement as soon as possible. Jot down everything you can remember as soon as you can after the meeting. Otherwise, it is easy to forget some of the details.

Although you may feel that one person is being a real stickler and very annoying, try to be patient. If the other side says it is important to them, try to work something out so the negotiations can be finalized. If the other side wants an answer for every possible contingency, it can easily bog down the process. Sometimes you have to agree in "principle" and leave the details to another day. It is a good thing to get all the i's dotted and the t's crossed. It is better to have any misinterpretations cleared up now rather than later. You don't want a grievance to be filed because a misplaced comma changed the whole meaning of the sentence.

Script:

This is an important item and the language must be exactly right in order for me to approve it. We must have all the T's crossed and the I's dotted.

Since we do not have time to work out all the details, let's write down the areas where we agree so we can work on this the next time.

I know it is important to work out contingencies so we don't come back to the bargaining table. However, let's work on the one or two that are most likely to occur and wait and see how this new policy works. Why spend a lot of time on something that probably will never happen?

RULE 39 KNOW WHEN TO CLOSE OR WHEN TO FOLD

An impasse occurs when the parties are deadlocked and there does not appear to be any room for agreement. You have come to a point where both parties are ready to throw in the towel. At this point there are a few strategies that might help to chip away at the impasse. If emotions are high and both parties are clearly frustrated and tired, it might be time for a break. Try to clear the air and get a fresh start the next day or the next week. When you get back together, this is the time to emphasize mutual interests and stress the cost of not agreeing. This might also be a time to try to agree in principle and work out the specifics at a later time. It is also a good time to brainstorm to discuss solutions without making any decisions or commitments. Even humor can help with a funny story to relieve the tension of the deadlock. Using "What If?" can also help by showing the consequences of not getting an agreement. Using a deadline might help, but be careful doing this unless you think that this will help move things along.

Just as the song says, you need to know when to close the negotiations. Some things will never be resolved. When you have reached an impasse and have done everything you can think of to break the deadlock, it may be time to think of folding. If you have made several suggestions which were not met with any discussion or interest, this may be one of those situations that won't get resolved. On the other hand, if you are moving very slowly but still talking to each other and making some progress, albeit at a snail's pace, it might be worthwhile to still plod away.

Not only is it important to know when to close the deal, it is also crucial to know how to close the deal. Otherwise a negotiation can go on and on and never get resolved. You may want to go to a package deal to start wrapping things up. If you just have nothing more to give, you need to tell the other side that there is nothing else to squeeze from you.

I would not say this is my "final" offer, but we are getting very close to that.

It looks as though we have reached a deadlock. Let's take a break for a week. So we can look at this impasse with fresh eyes.

Let's take a look at what will happen if we cannot resolve this situation ourselves. First it will take the decision out of our hands. Secondly, the employees will not get paid for at least six months. Third, neither party may get what it wants. Maybe it is worth another look to see if there is anything we have overlooked.

Keep track of the paperwork.

Keeping track of the paperwork is always important, but it is especially important when you are on the phone. That person on the other end of the line can easily be lost forever if you do not get contact information at the beginning of the call. That is a good safeguard in case the connection is lost. It is also a good idea to get the other side's correct telephone number, especially if you were transferred two or three times. You need to keep track of all calls, with the customer service rep's name, number, and the telephone transaction number, if there is one. In addition write down everything that was promised. Also ask for the rep's email and postal address so that you can send a follow-up email or letter describing what was said, what was promised, and when it was promised. This will be useful if you need to call again if the rep does not do what was promised. At that point, go as high on the chain of command as you can with your complaint.

Be Careful what you say and how you say it.

Prepare what you are going to say and if necessary, read from your written notes, since the other side cannot see you. Be sure to say everything that you want to say while the other party is on the phone. It may be difficult to get the same party the next time you call. It is best to get all your arguments on the table with one person. It is particularly important not to talk off the cuff. Be courteous when you call and try to control your frustration and anger, at least in the beginning, to see what they can do for you. It is probably not in your best interests to yell at the person on the other line.

Remember that the customer service rep is there for you. If you alienate the rep, she will be less inclined to help you. The customer rep is usually not the one at fault so it is not really fair to get mad at him or her. Remember that calls may be recorded for customer service purposes. If there are records of your call, that is another reason to be polite and charming.

B. HOW TO NEGOTIATE ONLINE

Negotiating online has some fundamental differences from negotiating in person. First of all, it is not done extemporaneously, negotiations online are by definition a delayed process. One party sends an email and then waits for a response. Like telephone negotiations, you cannot see the person and in addition cannot hear the person. You are getting all your cues from the online message. This has both pros and cons. It is hard to get used to in the beginning, but in a way you cannot make any judgments about the person and is somewhat freeing.

There are certain etiquette rules when typing online. ALL CAPS ARE NOT TO BE USED. This is like shouting in a face to face negotiation and is considered very rude. Once an email message has been sent, it cannot be taken away. Be careful of your tone. Somehow the bald language without inflection or visual cues accentuates the meaning of the language. For example, a joke or a funny remark may go flat when the other side sees it because they cannot hear your inflection when reading it. The other side might even be insulted. Being online is much more literal. Be careful with typos and misspellings. If your English is not proper, it can distract from your message. Because you are typing and thinking at the same time, it is easy to make mistakes which only get noticed after you have already sent it.

Don't send a message immediately after you have written it. Use spell checker and grammar checker. However this is not fail-proof because you may have written a legitimate word and the spell checker will not pick it up even though it is not the word that you intended. People have a chance to study what you have written. In a face to face negotiation, the other side quickly forgets exactly what was said, but in online negotiation done with a series of emails, either party can go back and see exactly what was said.

Negotiating online is much more exacting than negotiating in person. It is important not to act hastily after receiving a message especially if you are angry about something the other side said and you want to send back a sarcastic or angry email. Go ahead and write it out, but don't send it yet. Sleep on it and then review your email the next day before you decide whether to send it or not or whether to tone it down.

Most of the same principles found in Rules above can be used, but be aware of the differences from real time negotiating. Here are some of the rules that apply online.

Set the tone

When you are sending your messages by email, that is the only thing the other side sees. The other party cannot see your face or look at your body language. Your emails will set the tone. Do not write everything in capital letters. This is like shouting. Be careful with expressions like LOL (laughing out loud), smiley faces, funny noises or anything else that might be amusing with your friends, but not professional when setting the tone for a negotiation

Say what you want.

This is particularly appropriate for online negotiation because you are dealing with emails. You cannot hem and haw as you might in person. You must be clear and direct so there are no misunderstandings.

When you are negotiating online with emails, be careful what you write and how you write it. As mentioned above, you have to be more careful when you type emails because either party can easily pull up a copy of what is said. Emails can sound cold to the reader so be careful not to be too clinical. Trying to be comical can fall flat so try to keep an even tone. It is very important to proofread and double check everything before it goes out. If you have read some of your emails after the fact, you know that it is easy to make typing mistakes and they are not easily spotted when you do your first proofread. Remember, everyone needs an editor. In an important or complex negotiation, it is a good idea to put away your initial email and review it the next day for errors before sending it out. Once you have sent it, it is too late. You can create more problems if you are dealing with damage control with an email full of mistakes and typos. The other side can also be offended if the email looks carelessly written because of all the grammar and spelling errors. It sets a tone that you don't care and are not professional.

Keep track of the paperwork

This is even more important when communicating online. The emails are easily available so be careful to keep accurate track of offers and counter-offers to stay on track. If you don't, the other side will, and you may be embarrassed if they have to correct you.

Don't give anything away without getting something

Now that you are sending messages via email, don't forget that this is still a negotiation. Don't be lulled into forgetting some of the basic premises of negotiation such as not giving away something without getting something. It may be easy to chat online but focus on your goal and use the same negotiation techniques. You still need to get something anytime you give something away.

Don't rush or be too slow; know the rhythm

The rhythm of an online negotiation is very different from being in the same room. You have to set the pace. Don't be too slow by not answering the emails in a timely manner. If one party takes days or even weeks to answer an email, it can make the pace so slow that parties lose interest altogether. On the other hand, don't make it look as though you are waiting at your computer for the other side's next message. Even if you feel you are on a roll, put some distance in time between messages. You do not want to appear too eager. The other party may think that you are desperate to settle. Once you send some emails back and forth, you will develop your own online rhythm.

6

SPECIALIZED NEGOTIATIONS

The Rules so far have been a template for negotiations in general. However, there may be some special considerations depending on the type of negotiations. We negotiate every day even if we are not always aware of it. We negotiate as consumers. We may make purchases such as cars and homes where we are negotiating price. We stay in hotels or eat in restaurants and negotiate customer service. We deal with banks, credit card companies and insurance companies and are constantly on the phone trying to negotiate. We buy online through eBay or a website and have to negotiate broken or lost items.

We negotiate in the workplace. As employees we may not feel we have equal footing with the boss, but we negotiate our hours of work, our vacations, our salaries, our training, our promotions and even our discipline and termination. As bosses, we negotiate with our employees to try to make them more productive. We work with them to do certain things and reward them with conferences, raises or promotions. We discipline them with demotions, suspensions or even termination.

We negotiate with our families, too. We negotiate with our spouses, parents and siblings. Even our young children are negotiating how late they stay up, what television program they get to watch, or even whether they can have an ice cream before going to bed. Even in the professional arena of medicine and law, we negotiate fees and hourly rates

I have some chosen the following special negotiations and have suggested some of the rules to be used in each one.

A. How to negotiate with your boss

B. How to negotiate with an ex-Spouse

C. How to negotiate a good rate at a hotel

D. How to negotiate on Ebay.

After you get started, you will see that the rules are basically the same and can be adjusted for every situation. Soon you will be negotiating like a professional.

A. How to Negotiate with your Boss

Negotiating with your boss can be a little tricky because you are not on an equal footing. Since there is always the chance there could be repercussions for speaking out, an employee usually won't tell his boss what he is really thinking. Anyway let's assume that you want to get a raise or a promotion. Here are some of the rules you can use to negotiate with your boss.

Focus on the goal; don't be distracted by emotions

It is especially important not to let your emotions interfere with a request to your boss. If you are angry because you were passed over for a promotion or did not get the raise you think you deserved, it is not a good idea to immediately go to your boss's office and demand a meeting. You will appear to be out of control, which you probably are, and the boss will probably be glad he made the decision he did.

The best thing you can do is use that adrenalin rush and start writing down everything you would like to tell the boss about why you deserved the promotion or raise. Write down everything you can remember about what you were told about what you had to do to get one. Compile all records such as letters, emails or a calendar or diary of your meetings, so you can review them when you are ready to prepare the rebuttal for your boss.

You don't have to like your boss to negotiate with him.

It does not matter if you don't like your boss or if some of his traits are irritating. It is unlikely that he is going to change. You can, however, negotiate with your boss. You cannot let your dislike for your boss interfere with your request for a meeting for a raise or promotion. You need to separate the raise from the person. It is also important not to assume the outcome is negative. Don't tell your-self, "What is the use? He does not like me and no matter what I say, he is not going to change his mind!" That is self-defeating and if you really believe that, there is no point in trying to change your boss's decision. You need to put your feelings about your boss aside and negotiate with him the way you would if you liked him.

Know what you want

It is very important that you know what you want when you speak with your boss about a wage increase or any other benefit. If the boss asks you," How much do you want?" you need to have an answer rehearsed. This is not a time to hesitate unless you are caught completely off-guard. Be careful with the figure that you give him. Don't make it too little so you that you kick yourself later on for not asking for more. Don't make it too much so the boss thinks that you are greedy and unrealistic. If you are asked why you deserve the raise, do not say, *"I don't know"*. This needs to be rehearsed as well so that you can give a reasoned answer anytime anyplace.

Know what you are worth

Before you tell your boss how much you want, you need to do as much research as possible before the meeting. Find out what others in comparable positions are making at your company. This can be difficult in a private company but is usually available in the public sector. Each state's sunshine (open government) laws are different. For example Florida law is very liberal and public salaries are available to anyone who requests the employer for this information. When you get the information, then you need to analyze it. For example, if the person you are comparing yourself to has five more years of service, then you need to factor that in. County or state information might also be helpful. It depends on the position itself. A City Manager position would probably look to other cities in the county and possibly other counties nearby of the same size. Read the employee handbook to see if there is a policy pertinent to salary review and evaluations. Be aware of the timeframes and requirements and appeal process, if any. You don't want to find out later that you missed a deadline.

Have a Plan B

If you have had your heart set on getting a raise or promotion, you still need to have a Plan B. First you have to decide whether you are going to stay in the position anyway or start looking for a new job if you don't get the raise or promotion. Even if you decide that you are going to look for a new job, don't be too quick to quit the old job. However, you may want to look at your job in a new light and decide that whatever experience you get from now on should help you prepare for a new job. If you get tuition remission, you may have to pay back for the classes if you don't stay the requisite time on the job. However, if you get a new job, you probably won't care. You may want to consider taking classes online to improve your skills.

You might want to volunteer for projects at your company that are outside your field of expertise or comfort zone so that you can widen your experience on your resume. Sometimes the Plan B is a lot harder to determine than Plan A. A lot of time and energy has been invested in moving forward in your company. When Plan A falls apart, it can be emotionally devastating. It is always good to have developed Plan B, C and D just in case the others do not work out. When you are dealing with your livelihood, it can be very disheartening to try to figure out alternatives. If you have made a decision to leave the company, you should definitely know what Plan B is before quitting or threatening to quit Plan A.

What is important to you may not be important to your boss.

Your raise or promotion is very important to you but may not be very important to your boss. Having a meeting with you might be annoying, uncomfortable, boring, or even economically unadvisable. You are going to be well prepared for your meeting. However, your boss may not even have read your file and instead of thinking about your problems, he might be thinking about his career and his problems at home. He may have instructions from his bosses as to the number of personnel and the overall budget increases and may feel that his hands are tied regarding your situation. He may even agree that you deserve a raise but he has to go by the party line. You need to be aware of these possibilities or distractions and not be flustered when your boss is not overwhelmed by your logic and knowledge.

Never give or take no for an answer

Your boss may tell you right away that you are not getting a promotion or raise. If you accept that you are not getting it, then that is the end of the meeting. Perhaps you can suggest some alternatives. If you don't get the promotion, maybe you can at least get a raise. Ask for another meeting to discuss the issues discussed. Can you get a provisional promotion and if it does not work out, you will go back to your current job? Can they give you the duties of the new position and not give you a raise for six months? Maybe you could ask for something else instead of a raise such as extra vacation days. As you can see, there are endless possibilities. If you can suggest some to your boss, maybe one will stick. If your boss still says no, then you may have to go to Plan B.

It doesn't hurt to ask. If you don't ask you don't get.

You may think that your employer is not going to agree to anything you suggest, but the worst thing they could say is *"no"*. You never really know until you ask and you might be pleasantly surprised. You have nothing to lose and the boss might appreciate your ingenuity or persistence. Some things you might request at work are telecommuting, extended leave of absence, training course, new computer, corner office, flexible time, extended hours, more work, less work, membership in a professional organization, or travel to a national conference. The list is endless and only limited by your imagination. However, don't overdo it so that you ask for something every time you speak with your boss. A good time to ask is when you have done well on an assignment.

Walk Away

There may be instances where you decide that you have to just walk away. If the boss is not willing to make you partner or give you the raise you thought you deserved, you may decide that this not the boss or company you want to work for anymore. Just make sure this decision is not made in haste while you are still angry about your boss' decision. If you do walk away, have a plan so you know how you will proceed. It is the conventional wisdom that it is harder to find a job when you no longer have one. Give yourself some time to make this final decision. You do not want to come into your boss's office on a Monday morning and beg for your job back. You would not be in a position of strength.

Step back and look at the big picture

When something happens at work like not getting a raise or partnership, it is a good time to reflect on the big picture. Can I stay here and work out these issues with my boss? Or is this a good time to throw in the towel and go with another company or with another type of employment? Where do I want to be five years from now or fifteen years from now? Do I want to be self-employed where I make my own decisions? Was this really a blessing in disguise? Am I better off knowing now that this job is not for me so I can go in another direction with my life? Your answers to these questions will help you decide the direction of your next move.

B. How to Negotiate with a Spouse or Ex-Spouse

It can be difficult negotiating with a current spouse because you will still live in the same house after the negotiations are over. A certain amount of decorum and sensitivity is needed. Negotiating with an ex-spouse is difficult because of the emotional elements. Most people don't like their ex-spouses; otherwise they would probably still be married.

Here are some rules for negotiating with ex-spouses.

Focus on the goal; don't be distracted by emotions

Dealing with an ex-spouse can be very emotional. It is very important to focus on the particular goal. For example, let's say you are figuring out a yearly schedule for vacations and weekends between spouses and your agreement is 50–50. If you start to argue about something else, always come back to the goal of completing the schedule.

You can negotiate with a lunatic

Just because you don't like your ex-spouse and your ex-spouse does not like you, doesn't mean that you can't still negotiate with him about the schedule. It won't be easy but try to set your animosity aside while working on the calendar.

Look forward, not back. The past is the past for a reason.

Don't let arguments in the past enter into the discussion today. If your ex-spouse makes a snide remark or criticizes you, try to ignore it. You are meeting to discuss this year's calendar not last year's problems.

Know what you want

Know in advance what weekends you want. Know all the dates you are requesting to have custody such as vacations and birthdays and those days you don't want custody because you are going to be away for business. Don't tell the other side yet what your preference is.

Request Ground Rules

If previous discussions have been ugly, you may want to suggest some ground rules to make the process go more smoothly. For example you may want to agree on the procedure for picking days. Do you go month by month or take turns picking days throughout the year? If you cannot decide on a process in advance, it will be chaotic and take forever. You may want to have some ground rules for behavior. One person will be allowed to speak without interruption. There should also be ground rules for dealing with changes in the calendar during the year and the proper notification of the other spouse.

Volunteer

You have to make a judgment call as to whether it is an advantage for you to do the first draft or for your ex-spouse to do one. This might be a good time to volunteer to do a first draft of the schedule. Usually it is an advantage to do a draft. The other side may not want to take the time to do it. Expect lots of criticism. If you let the other side do it and there are problems, you can point out that it is his handiwork and he signed off on it. This is your call. If you do it, you will be able influence the methodology of picking the days.

Agree on the issues and prioritize them

You both need to prioritize your preferred days. If you do the first draft, you can recommend a system of taking each side's first priority and putting it on the calendar and then taking the other side's first priority. When there is an overlap, then you can have some discussion about deciding who gets the days. The more you can make an automatic procedure or system, the easier the negotiation will be.

Anticipate what the other side wants.

You need to anticipate what your ex-spouse wants. You probably already know the birthdays or other important days. Try to figure it out as much as possible so you can fit that into your schedule.

Don't gloat

If you get something you want, don't gloat. There is nothing worse than seeing an ex-spouse gloat or smirk. The other side will want to take that expression off your face and will try to retaliate. Go through these negotiations with a poker face.

Tradeoff or split the difference

There may be chances for a simple tradeoff. You take back that weekend and I will give you this weekend. Don't expect the dynamics to be simple. When you do these tradeoffs, don't make them unwieldy or inconvenient for your children. One day here and one day there just because their parents could not agree is not fair to the children.

Watch the other side's body language

You lived with this person and you should be able to read his/her body language. Use this information to your advantage. If you see that vein in his forehead bulging, you may know he is very upset. If he is thumping his fingers on the counter, you may know he is impatient and bored. Try to use these moods to your advantage. If he is mad, it might not be the best time to talk about the Christmas Holidays. If he is getting impatient, maybe you can wrap it up.

Don't expect thanks or gratitude when it is all over.

If you were the one who did the drafts and graphs and spent a lot of time on various drafts of the calendar, don't expect any thanks or gratitude. Just be glad the calendar is finished.

C. HOW TO NEGOTIATE WITH A HOTEL

Negotiating with a hotel is usually not as emotionally-charged as negotiating with your boss or spouse. However, if you have just had a long flight and you come into a hotel and find that your reservation has been given to someone else, that is a different matter. The same rules would also apply to restaurants and most other customer service establishments. Here are some rules to use when negotiating with hotels.

Do your research

When you call to make a reservation you should have already done your research. What is the rate online? What discounts can you use, AARP or AAA? Are there promotions? Are their special week-end or weekday rates? You can go online and get commentary from other consumers or recommendations from guide books. How many stars does it have? Call more than once so that you can see if you get different quotes. If you get an offer online or on the phone that seems too good to be true, make your reservation immediately so that you don't lose the rate.

Only Negotiate with someone with authority

When looking for a good rate, it might be better to deal directly with the front desk instead of online or through the hotels' websites. Individual hotel managers have authority to be more flexible in rates. The online rates usually cannot be altered. You should also check rates at nearby hotels and comparable hotels. It is always good to know comparables. If you have a problem at the desk or while staying at the hotel, it is always a good idea to ask for the manager. Again this may be the only person to have the authority to give you something for your inconvenience such as an upgrade or free room.

If you don't ask, you don't get

When calling on the phone or asking at the desk, try to probe for a better deal. They usually won't offer outright, so you need to ask the right questions. You could ask these questions. "Is that the best you can do?" "Do you have any specials?", "If you cannot lower the price, can you give me an upgrade?"

Keep track of the paperwork

Once you get your reservation, make sure that you get your confirmation number, and the name of the reservationist. You might want to call a few days later to make sure you still have that great rate. If you have problems at the hotel, keep copious notes of what went wrong, when it went wrong, and the names of employees who helped you or did not help you.

Walk away

If you are not getting any response about getting a good rate, you might mention what the rate is next door or on a similar property. If you use this technique, be prepared to walk away to keep the regular rate if the rate is not reduced. If you had a bad experience at the hotel and you want to lodge a complaint, write directly to the Manager of the hotel since they have the authority to offer you something. Be sure you have all the facts and times and names of those involved. While on a plane on the way home, jot down everything you can remember about the problem. When you write this letter, you may want to say how upsetting it was for you. Keeping your cool is not as important with a hotel as it might be with your boss or spouse. Be sure to state what you want. Do you want a certificate for one free room or just an apology? If you do not get an answer from the hotel manager, then send copies of the letter to the customer service department or to the president of the company.

D. How to negotiate on Ebay

1) What is eBay and how does it work?

EBay (See Glossary) is an online auction for sellers to sell their items to buyers and buyers to buy from sellers. It uses an automatic bidding system to make bidding on auctions more convenient and less time consuming. When you make a bid, you enter the maximum amount you'd be willing to pay. This information is kept confidential and not divulged to buyers or sellers. The eBay system compares your bids to any other bids on the item and in effect, the system places bids on your behalf. It uses only as much of your bid as is needed to be the highest bidder. If another bidder has a higher amount, then you will be outbid and you have the opportunity to make a higher bid.

Here is an example of how it works. You see a Fender guitar that you want to bid on. The maximum you are willing to bid is $300. The minimum bid is $50. If someone else has already secretly bid over $300, then you will get a message that you have been outbid. If the highest bid before you bid was $200, your bid will be shown at the next increment or $205.00. If no one else bids, then you will get the item for the $205 not the $300.

EBay has revolutionized how people buy and sell antiques, collectibles and even new items. EBay does not handle the item; it only provides the online framework to bid and charges insertion fees and a percentage commission of the final bid. EBay has its own rules and if you are not familiar with eBay or are a newbie (new to eBay), you may want to browse their website at www.ebay.com. You could buy a penny item or a $100,000 car, but the concepts are basically the same regardless of the value of the item.

2) What is feedback?

Negotiating with an eBay buyer or seller has many dimensions. First there is feedback, which is a way to evaluate a member's reputation and the backbone of the eBay process. For each eBay transaction, the buyer and seller are allowed to rate each other by leaving a rating of positive, neutral, or negative. A positive gets a 1, a neutral 0 and a negative—1. A glance at the eBay member's profile shows the total in each of the three categories and the total percentage of positives. Of course, 100 % is the best percentage, but if some one has 98 or 99 %, you know that there were only a very few unsatisfied customers. However if the score is below zero and the person has a history of neutral and negative feedbacks, then that is notice to the other party to be prudent in dealing with this buyer or seller.

If the negative feedback happened a long time ago, that is a positive sign. If there are several recent negative feedbacks, that is a warning to anyone not to bid on their items. If you decide to bid anyway and you have problems, you cannot say you were not warned. EBay users are very proud of feedback and can become very upset if someone gives them a negative rating especially if they think it is unjustified. If someone has a perfect rating of 100%, that individual may go to great lengths to have that feedback withdrawn to get back their perfect score.

3) How can negative feedback be withdrawn?

If both parties agree that feedback should be withdrawn, then there is a mechanism through eBay to withdraw the feedback. See the Ebay website www.ebay.com . Often in the heat of the moment a party may say something that they are willing to withdraw after their anger subsides. Feedback is no longer *removed;* it is only *withdrawn (*unless the feedback contains objectionable language such as lewdness or profanity, which will be removed by eBay). That means that anyone can still see the feedback, but the negative rating is changed for that one eBay transaction. If the parties cannot resolve their dispute themselves, then they can go to Squaretrade, which is a mediation service for eBay users. For a small fee, Squaretrade will select a mediator who will work with both parties by sending them separate emails and work as a facilitator to resolve their eBay dispute. The feedback can also be withdrawn through the mediation process.

Here are some of the rules that would be pertinent to negotiating on eBay.

Look forward not back. The past is the past for a reason

When you are dealing with someone on eBay, don't dwell on all that has gone wrong in the past such as, "you did not answer my emails; you did not send it on time". Get from the past to the present by asking what you can do to resolve the situation. You may want to let the other side vent, but getting mired in a blame game is not going to resolve your dispute. If receipt of emails was a problem, there might be a spam block preventing the messages from getting through.

When someone checks their spam folder, they can sometimes find these messages and will sometimes change their attitude toward the other party.

You don't have to be right to settle

If the buyer says something like "It is not the money, it is the principle" or the seller says something like, "I would not sell this to her after what she has done!." the dispute is unlikely to settle unless you can change the other party's mind set. Often feedback can be the leverage needed. Even though the other side does not want to deal with the other party in any way, their desire to have their feedback may supersede their *principles*.

Know what it is worth

This is particularly important when bidding on eBay. First of all you can see the final prices of other items that have sold on ebay. This is an invaluable tool to determine what your bid is. Be sure you are checking a comparable item. If you are looking at a coin that is uncirculated, it is not going to be worth the same as a proof coin. Be sure you are not comparing apples and oranges, but apples and apples. Also look at the condition of the item. If there are flaws such as cracks or dings or crazing, that can affect the value. Factor the value of repairs and flaws when bidding. Don't bid as though it was perfect. As a seller, you can get a reality check by looking at other eBay values.

You may think you have a rare and unusual item and would be willing to pay a premium for it in an antique shop. However, now that eBay is an international source of goods, there may be many items similar to yours for sale and that can deflate the price. It is a simple case of supply and demand. However, if there is something special about your item such as a low mintage or a rare year or a rare mint such as Carson City, your item may have special value over the other coins. If your item is a one of a kind item or is in pristine condition, buyers may be willing to pay a premium price because they know it might be a long time, if ever, when another item like it will be sold on eBay.

Does the other side want something other than money?

The other side may want your feedback withdrawn or an apology (both discussed above). You may have to put on your thinking cap to see what else you can offer. If the item is broken, you might arrange for someone to come to their home to repair it. This is particularly helpful in computer sales. You can always get a computer tech to take a look in the buyer's location. Usually the other side will be unwilling to take the time or spend the money to send an item back and then wait for you to determine what repairs are needed and then wait for its return. If you have another item or perhaps a slightly better item, you can offer to exchange the defective item. The other side may balk if you insist that they pay any additional shipping. If you are out of the ordered model, but you have a comparable or better one in stock, explain what the differences are so the buyer will know they are getting a better deal. Sometimes the other side just wants an explanation of what happened. If the item took three weeks to get to the buyer's house, what was the explanation? If the packing was not good and the item was broken, what happened?

Don't make promises you cannot keep.

If you know the shipping is going to be delayed, tell the buyer. Some buyers wait around their house all day waiting for delivery and when there is no delivery, they are furious. Always give your self some leeway when making promises. It is better for the buyer to be pleasantly surprised that the item arrived a day before you predicted rather than the other way around. If you know an item is out of stock, be realistic about the true delivery date. If you say you will help the buyer out, don't change your mind when you find out the cost or the time involved. If you cannot keep your promise, then don't make it in the first place.

Be willing to apologize

Being willing to apologize is particularly important in eBay transactions. When things go wrong, it is best to show some empathy and apologize for the inconvenience or miscommunication even if you believe it is the post office's fault for losing the package or the package arriving broken. For some people, it is hard to accept blame or responsibility when they know in their heart that they did nothing wrong. If you are this kind of person, just keep in mind that you are trying to get that feedback withdrawn and are willing to compromise in order to get that goal. Try to put yourself into the buyer's shoes who paid promptly for the item. It is not his fault either.

Everyone makes mistakes

No one is perfect and everyone makes mistakes. When you buy and sell on eBay, it is inevitable that there will be mistakes. It is just human nature. The seller will send item A to person B and item B to person A. After a package has been mailed, the seller finds the belt at home for the dress just shipped. Sometimes the best approach is to acknowledge that a mistake has been made and figure out how to undo the mistake and get on with your life instead of saying something like, "You were careless" or "You should have packed better." This way you skip the recriminations and go straight to a solution. If you are the one making the mistake, you should sincerely apologize and see how you can make it up to the other party.

Follow-up

Follow-up is very important in eBay auctions especially if you do not want negative feedback posted against you. Although it is frowned upon by eBay, some eBay buyers and sellers will leave feedback without contacting the other party and allowing them the opportunity to correct the situation. You want to do everything you can to prevent that from happening.

As an eBay seller, you need to communicate regularly with your buyers to keep them informed. They need to know how much money they owe, including postage and handling. They should be informed when payment is received and told when to expect the delivery and the method of shipping. I recommend getting tracking or at the very least delivery confirmation. The tracking is worth the expense. Both sides can check the tracking and will know if there is a delay and if it is the carrier's fault. If the item is lost and you do not have tracking, no one will know for sure what happened to the item.

The seller may suspect that the buyer received it and is lying. The buyer may suspect that the seller did not even ship the item at all. Keeping the buyer informed is good customer service and the buyer feels that he is being treated in a respectful way.

As an eBay buyer, you should read the whole listing and make sure that you have not missed any pertinent information such as a handling charge or price of shipping outside the U.S. When a buyer buyers two or more items from the same buyer, he usually expects the seller to allow him to combine shipping and save on postage by only shipping one package. If that is not the case, the listing should say so. Some sellers are a little sneaky and bury some of the details of the listing in the small print. You need to look for words like "refurbished", "like new" or "slightly used". The seller's idea of "like new" could be a lot different from the buyer's idea of "like new". If you do not read the listing carefully, which is in effect his offer to you, then you cannot complain afterwards. You have to live with what was in the listing. If you do have questions for the seller such as combining shipping costs, picking up the item, or questions about the condition of the item, then those issues should be addressed to the seller before the auction ends.

Beware and be aware

Whether you are buying or selling on Ebay, you must be prudent and use common sense, good judgment and caution. There are many scams and frauds on the internet so you want to protect yourself. Learn about the seller before bidding. See how many negative feedbacks and total positive feedbacks he has. If he has less than 10 feedbacks, he is either a 1) "newbie" (new on eBay) who does not have much knowledge of eBay or 2) he may have sold under a previous identity and recently started a new account with a different ID. The latter usually means that he had a lot of negative feedbacks on the old account and has opened a new account to get a fresh start. From the buyer's perspective it is usually not a good sign. It is also a good idea to look at eBay's Security Center at its website www.ebay.com to see what buyer protection plans are offered.

For example a good way to pay for an item is with a credit card. If the merchandise is not received by the buyer, you can put through a claim with the credit card company. Another good way to pay is through Paypal, which sends funds from a verified bank account or credit card directly to the seller online. Sellers who choose to send to a non-verified address will not be protected by Paypal's buyer protection system. For example, if someone is buying a gift, he might want the seller to send the item directly to the recipient. That kind of transaction would not be covered by a buyer protection plan because it was sent to a non-verified address. Cash should never be sent through the mail. There is no proof as to whether it was sent or received. There is no protection plan available for cash. An instant cash wire transfer, such as Western Union is not recommended by eBay because it cannot be traced and there is no recourse if the wire transfer is not received. For further information about EBay's Standard Purchase Protection Plan, See Ebay's Security Center at www.ebay.com. For more information about Paypal Protection Plan, see www.paypal.com.

In addition, do not ever give anyone your account information for paypal, eBay, Aol, a credit card or respond to any email that requests this information. It might look like an official email from eBay or paypal, but a scam artist is trying to get your account information and steal your identity so he can use your account and positive feedback to sell items on eBay or get funds from your paypal account. This is called an email "spoof" and the website you are lured to is a "phishing site". If you get such an email, you need to click forward and email to spoof@ebay.com or spoof@apaypal.com or a similar address for your bank and the appropriate security department will investigate. Don't even open these emails, but if you do, do not put in your account information. If you make a mistake and think that you may have been spoofed by one of these scams, contact eBay or paypal or your credit company immediately so they can close down your account before the account information is used. EBay has taken precautions so that all messages to eBay members are sent through their My Ebay site for each eBay user. The scammer's techniques are getting more advanced and sophisticated so you need to keep current online so you are not scammed by the next fraudulent scheme.

Don't expect thanks or gratitude when it is all over

You may feel that you have really gone out on a limb for an eBay customer. You made special allowances. You sent them a refund even though they did not send the item back. You sent the item federal express so that there would be no delay. You arranged pickup of the other item. You were pleasant and charming and did everything you could do to make the transaction satisfactory. When it was all, over, you heard nothing, not even an email. If you expect thanks, then most likely you will be disappointed.

7

WHAT HAPPENS WHEN NEGOTIATIONS FAIL?

A certain number of negotiations will reach impasse and that deadlock cannot be broken by the parties. You will need to make a decision as to whether you want to go to another forum such as mediation or arbitration, drop the case altogether or file a formal complaint.

SHOULD YOU GO TO MEDIATION?

If you have made some progress but don't like dealing with each other, it might be a good time to bring in a mediator, who can work with the parties in individual caucuses. The mediator will facilitate and the parties do not have to work with each other anymore.

Mediation is a process where parties use a neutral facilitator, a mediator, to help the parties resolve their dispute. The parties do not deal with each other directly; all communication goes through the mediator. Although the mediator will meet with both parties together, most of the work usually gets down in the caucus (See Glossary) when the mediator meets with one party alone. The caucus allows the parties to discuss the merits of the case with the mediator without the other party present. The parties can also tell the mediator in caucus what information to divulge, when to divulge it and what not to divulge. The caucus also allows the mediator be the devil's advocate (See Glossary) and to speak frankly and discuss the strengths and weaknesses of the dispute.

The mediator does not make a decision like a judge or arbitrator. However, if the parties agree, he can make suggestions or recommendations. Sometimes the parties have already tried to negotiate directly with the other party, but the negotiations reached an impasse or deadlock. When there is animosity between the parties, mediation can be successful because the mediator acts like a buffer between the two parties.

SHOULD YOU GO TO ARBITRATION?

If mediation does not work, you may want to consider arbitration. Arbitration takes away the control of resolving the issue themselves, but the arbitrator will make a decision based on the facts and evidence presented to her/him. The parties need to look at how much they are willing to spend and how important the final resolution is to them before deciding how to proceed.

Arbitration is a process where parties present their arguments in a hearing format to an arbitrator who makes the decision. The parties may have already tried to resolve it themselves through negotiation or mediation. By going to arbitration, they have given the decision-making power to the arbitrator, who acts as a judge. The arbitration hearing is much more informal than court. Arbitration can either be binding or nonbinding. Labor/Management arbitration is binding, which means that the decision cannot be appealed or overturned unless the Arbitrator showed bias or discrimination in his decision. The courts have long recognized that labor arbitrators have a specialized knowledge of labor law that judges generally do not have. An arbitration that is not biding means that the parties can reject the decision. The parties may not take a non-binding arbitration seriously if they have the power to reject the decision law that judges generally do not have.

Alternate Dispute Resolution (known as ADR), is an alternative to taking a case to court. Collectively, procedures such as negotiation, mediation, arbitration and med/arbitration are a cheaper and faster alternative to litigation. In addition, the parties have more control of the outcome of the case, especially in negotiation or mediation. If the parties must work with each other after the hearing, such as the parents in child custody or visitation cases, ADR is preferable than going to court. The rift and animosity between the parents may be increased as a result of an adversarial process.

SHOULD YOU GO TO MEDIATION/ ARBITRATION?

Mediation/arbitration known as med-arb is a hybrid process. An arbitrator is chosen, but if both parties agree, he will mediate the case first and then if that does not succeed, he will arbitrate the case and make a decision. The advantage is that you can have two processes done by the same person. The disadvantage is that the arbitrator may learn things about the case in the mediation phase that might affect the arbitration decision.

Online Dispute Resolution, known as ODR, is the online equivalent of Alternate Dispute Resolution. This is a way to resolve disputes online. Online Mediation services such as Squaretrade are used to resolve eBay disputes. Negotiating online is done via email and is not done in contemporaneous time like most ADR procedures. This is much different from face to face negotiating because you cannot see or hear the other party. Some strategies and techniques for online negotiating can be found in Chapter 5.

WHERE TO FILE A COMPLAINT

If you are dealing with a consumer transaction, you may have already tried to work it out directly with the seller, buyer or website operator. If you feel that fraud has been committed or you are the victim of a scam artist, you may want to file a complaint. There are agencies in each state and the Federal Fair Trade Commission that specialize in consumer protection. In deciding whether to pursue this, you need to weigh the amount of money lost and the time and energy you are willing to expend to see the claim through. For example, if you lost $50, that is probably not worth filing a claim. However if you lost $1000, then it is probably worthwhile. Remember that part of the purpose in filing is so that you can prevent other people from being defrauded.

Here are some Resources that you might contact:

1. The Attorney General's Office in your state.

2. The County or State Consumer Protection Agency

3. The Better Business Bureau in your community

4. The Federal Trade Commission. Their website is www.ftc.gov and call toll-free 1-877-FTC-Help, The FTC works for the consumer to prevent fraud, deception and unfair business practices in the marketplace. They also provide consumer information to help prevent consumer fraud. The FTC has a program called Consumer Sentinel, an online database, which enters these complaints such as Internet, telemarketing and identify theft and makes

them available to hundreds of civil and criminal law enforcement agencies in the US and abroad.

Appendix A

Glossary Terms

1. **Arbitration** is a process where parties present their arguments to a neutral arbitrator, and the arbitrator makes the decision. This is an alternative to litigation (going to court) and is one of the procedures known as Alternate Dispute Resolution, or ADR. Labor/Management Arbitration is one of the oldest kinds of arbitration. The Arbitrator is like a judge, while the parties make their own decisions in mediation and negotiation

2. **Alternate Dispute Resolution,** known as ADR, includes negotiation, mediation, and arbitration and other dispute procedures that are an alternative to going to court. Generally ADR is faster and less expensive than litigation. Generally the parties have more control of the outcome than if they filed a court case.

3. **Authority** means that the person negotiating has the authority or power to make a decision and act on behalf of his employer or company. Even if a person has authority, it might only be authority to a certain amount. It is better to know in the beginning what the person's authority is before the negotiations start. If someone does not have authority, then there is no point negotiating with them because they cannot approve any agreement.

4. **Bargaining Chip** is a concession that can be offered to the other side as an incentive to get something. Using the poker terminology makes the term a metaphor for the negotiation process. One should always keep some bargaining chips in reserve because they may be needed to close the deal.

5. **Boulewareism** is a *take it or leave it* approach to negotiation. The term is named after Lemuel Boulware, a vice-president at General Electric in the 1950's. After much research as to what was best for the company, he opened the negotiations with his first, last and best offer and told the electrical union

to *take it or leave it*. The court later determined that this one-sided approach was not good faith bargaining because there was no give and take by the parties and no involvement by the union. (This is sometimes spelled **Boulewarism**)

6. **Caucuses** are meetings held by a mediator separately with each party to discuss the mediation. It allows the party to talk about the dispute without the other party being present.

7. **Concession** is giving something up that the other party wants or agreeing with the other party. The term is used synonymously with bargaining chip. *You made too many concessions and don't have any bargaining chips left.*

8. **Confidentiality** means that information concerning the negotiation is not divulged or discussed with outside parties during the negotiations. This can jeopardize the negotiation process. It is important to make confidentiality part of the ground rules for the negotiation. It is also important all team members understand their obligations concerning confidentiality.

9. **Decoys** are used to mislead and lure an unsuspecting bird by setting out a realistic duck model so the bird will follow the decoy and allow hunters to shoot at him. This same tactic is used in negotiations. The purpose is to mislead the other unsuspecting party with a diversionary tactic which is the decoy. This is similar to the **smoke screen** and **red herring**.

10. **Devil's Advocate** is an approach used to give a reality check to the other side and point out the flaws in their arguments. The expression is *Let me play the devil's advocate.* By playing, one is insulated from criticism because you would only pointing out these problems if you were the devil.

11. **Face-saving** is a way to allow someone to get out of an embarrassing situation with their dignity intact. Giving someone a way out is a tradition in many Asian countries. You are helping the other side not look bad and be humiliated.

12. **Feedback** is a system that allows eBay users to rate the buyer or seller in each ebay transaction. A buyer or seller can leave a positive, neutral or negative rating and a comment to explain their satisfaction level. The feedback score is the sum of all of the ratings an ebay user received from individual users.

The positive number is compared to the negative to give the user a percentage number as well. For example, a perfect score of all positives is 100%.

13. **Final offer** is the last offer made in a negotiation. Don't call it a *final offer* if you have anything else to negotiate. Do not use the final offer at the beginning of negotiations; that would be Boulwareism, or a take or leave it approach There should only be one *final offer* and it should be a tool at the end of negotiations to close the deal.(See **Boulewarism** and **take it or leave it**)

14. **Good faith bargaining** is required by federal and state labor laws. It means that the parties have a duty to approach bargaining with the right attitude and are prepared to discuss issues and meet on a regular basis. It does not mean that the parties have to come to an agreement though. Good faith bargaining is the opposite of **Boulwareism** and **take it or leave it.**

15. **Groundrules** are the procedural rules that are used for the negotiation process and agreed to by both parties. Here are some examples: *Only one person will speak at a time and parties will be courteous at all times. Only the Spokesperson can speak on behalf of the team.* Having groundrules helps the negotiation run more smoothly because all parties know the expectations in advance.

16. **Impasse** occurs when the parties are deadlocked and there does not appear to be any room for agreement. The impasse has to be broken or the negotiation will have to close without resolution.

17. **Mediation** is a process where parties use a neutral facilitator called a mediator to help the parties resolve their dispute. The parties do not deal with each other directly as in a **negotiation.** The mediator does not make a decision as an **arbitrator** or judge does. The parties resolve the case with the mediator's assistance. Mediation is a type of **Alternate Dispute Resolution,** which is an alternative to going to court.

18. **Mediation/Arbitration,** known as Med/Arb, is a hybrid process. An arbitrator is chosen, but if both parties agree, he will mediate the case first and then if that does not succeed, he will arbitrate the case and make a decision. The advantage is that you can have two processes done by the same person. The disadvantage is that the arbitrator may learn things about the case in the mediation phase that might affect the arbitration decision.

19. **Negotiation** is a process where parties resolve disputes with each other. The term is often used synonymously with collective bargaining. The essence of the negotiations is that both parties agree to work with each other to resolve a problem of dispute. Negotiation is a type of **Alternate Dispute Resolution**, which is an alternative to going to court.

20. **Negotiating against oneself** occurs when you make another offer when there already is an offer on the table. You should always wait for a counter-offer or you will be negotiating against yourself. For example, you offer $5000 and then you offer $10,000. when the other party nodded "no". You should have asked for a counter-offer instead. The other party might have countered with $7500 and you have already lost $2500.

21. **Online Dispute Resolution,** known as **ODR,** is a way to resolve disputes online and is the online equivalent of **Alternate Dispute Resolution.** Online mediation is the most common form of ODR, but there is negotiation and arbitration as well. Online mediation is not done in real time like face to face mediation. ODR uses technology and its usage will increase and be as common as regular ADR

22. **Package Offer** is a way to put several proposals on the table to make the deal look more attractive. I will give you A, B and C, but we want D and E. This is sometimes called **Bundling** and is more complex than a **trade-off.**

23. **Phishing** is a fake website. Internet users are lured through lookalike emails from aol, paypal, eBay and banks asking for confidential account information. That information is used to access someone's account and steal their identity.

24. **Quid pro quo** means *this for that* literally in Latin. In negotiations, it means *I will give you what you want if you give me what I want.* It is basically the same as a **tradeoff**. Both parties can get what they want and the problem is solved.

25. **Red herring** is a tactic to mislead the other party and crate a diversion. The origin of the term involved rubbing a red herring on hounds to protect the hunted fox. The hounds will smell the herring and won't be able to track the fox. A red herring is essentially a false clue or phony issue used to distract hounds, politicians and negotiators. This is similar to **decoy** and **smoke screen**

26. **Saving Face** is a way to allow someone their dignity and not be humiliated

27. **Smoke screen** is a way to mask your true intent and create a diversion. In war, smoke is released to mask the location or moving of troops. In negotiations, it is a a diversionary tactic to take attention away from the main objective and give attention to something of little or not importance. This is similar to the **decoy** and **red herring.**

28. **Spoof** is an internet based scheme to steal someone's identity. An email is sent that looks like an official email from eBay, a bank, paypal or Aol, which lures the person to a fake website (phishing) with the purpose of tricking that person to giving confidential account information

29. **Take it or leave it** is an approach used to give the other side a first, last and firm offer and tell them you are not going to negotiate with them any longer) This is a risky approach especially at the beginning of negotiations. It should only be used at the end of negotiations to close the deal.(See **final offer** and **Boulwareism**)

30. **Tradeoff** is the same as **quid pro quo,** In negotiations, it means *I will give you what you want if you give me what I want.* Both parties can get what they want and the problem is solved

31. **Tentative Agreement,** known as a **TA,** is used as a way to tentatively agree on each proposal. It is understood that changes could still be made in the final version, but it is a good faith method to keep track of what has been agreed to.

32. **Venting** is a way to clear the emotions like anger and frustration so you can be ready for bargaining. It is a way to let go like screaming. By expressing your emotions, it clears the way for negotiations to take place. Often the first session of a negotiation or mediation will let the parties vent so that the procedure can go to the next step.

33. **Walkaway** is a variation of *take it or leave it.* If you don't give me what I want, then I will quit or walk away.

34. **Unfair Labor Practice** is a violation of federal or state labor law.

Appendix B

WHAT MAKES A GOOD NEGOTIATOR?

1. Calm, Cool, Collected

2. Creative

3. Ethical

4. Fair

5. Firm

6. Flexible

7. Good Listener

8. Honest

9. Knowledgeable

10. Patient

11. Perceptive

12. Persistent

13. Personable

14. Perceptive

15. Reasonable

16. Respectful

17. Sense of Humor

18. Sincere

19. Thinks Before Speaking

Appendix C

Do's and Don'ts of Negotiators

DO'S

1. Be Appreciative of time and effort

2. Be Calm

3. Be Confident

4. Be Confidential

5. Be in Control

6. Be Courteous

7. Be Flexible

8. Be a Good Listener

9. Delay if Necessary

10. Be Honest

11. Be Positive

12. Be Prepared

13. Be Tactful

14. Be United if you are part of a team

15. Have a Poker Face

16. Keep Session on Track

17. Read between the lines

DON'T

1. Argue with staff or team

2. Assume

3. Badmouth the other side

4. Blame

5. Be Afraid to Keep an issue on the Table

6. Be Defensive

7. Be Patronizing

8. Be Pressured

9. Compromise your principles

10. Escalate Demands

11. Interrupt

12. Keep worrying about the finished product

13. Let Down Your Guard

14. Lie

15. Lose Your Temper

16. Make Promises you cannot keep

17. React to your mistakes

18. Rush the other side

19. Reject alternatives offered until studied

20. Oversell

21. Underestimate the other side

22. Wait to Break Bad News

Appendix D
Ground Rules Sample Policy

Two Party Ground rules

1. Preliminaries: location, table set up, number of negotiators, cell phone rules

2. Agenda for each meeting

3. Everyone will speak with courtesy and there will be no profanity.

4. Meetings will start on time.

5. Meetings will last about four hours unless agreed otherwise

6. Proposals will be submitted in writing at the second meeting

7. Those topics or sections to be negotiated will be selected by the fourth meeting.

8. Either party can call a caucus whenever it wishes but will let the other party know if it will last more than twenty minutes.

9. Both parties agree to exchange information and comply with reasonable requests for information. The arty requesting the information agrees to pay reasonable reproduction costs.

10. The parties agree to discuss and confirm the date of their next negotiation sessions at the close of every session.

Negotiating Team Ground rules

1. Chief Negotiator is chief spokesperson

2. Chief spokesperson is only person authorized to accept or reject proposals and to make proposals or counter-proposals

3. Everyone speaks through chief spokesperson

4. Each team member has role

5. Nothing is discussed about negotiations except to team

6. If team member wants to speak, write a note to call a caucus

7. Keep negotiations materials secure

8. All team members attend all negotiation sessions.

9. Do not discuss something at a session unless team has already agreed.

978-0-595-39733-4
0-595-39733-6

Printed in the United States
53696LVS00005B/274-402